# Game Project Completed

*How Successful Indie Game Developers
Finish Their Projects*

By Thomas Schwarzl

Copyright © Thomas Schwarzl, 2014

All rights reserved


ISBN-13: 978-1490555454

# Table of Contents

## Introduction ................................................. 7
- Motivation ............................................. 8
- Audience .............................................. 8
- What You Will Find in This Book ......................... 9
- What You Won't Find in This Book .................... 10
- Personal Stories ................................... 11
- Gender ............................................. 11

## Going Indie ............................................. 13
- The Dream of Overnight Success ..................... 14
- Screw Small Games, Mine Will Be Epic! ........... 16
- Beginning, Disillusion and Transformation ........ 18
- Better or Different ................................. 19
- Choose the Right Idols ........................ 21
- Don't Think, Do ................................. 23
- The Nay-Sayers ................................. 26

## From Slave to Master ................................. 29
- You Get Paid per Sale, Not per Hour ............... 30
- Have Goals ....................................... 31
- Focus .............................................. 32
- Reduce Context Switching ................................. 35
- Keep a Work Journal ................................. 36
- Restrict Yourself ................................. 38
- Seek & Destroy Bottlenecks ............................. 41

| | |
|---|---|
| The Curse of Do It Yourself | 43 |
| Getting Better by Intention | 44 |
| Security | 46 |

## Agility  49

| | |
|---|---|
| Scrum 101 | 50 |
| Accept Imperfection | 53 |
| The Pareto Principle | 53 |
| Parkinson's Law | 55 |
| Get Yourself an Agile Mindset | 56 |
| Start Lean | 58 |
| Plans Are Worthless, Planning Is Everything | 60 |
| Software Is Organic | 60 |
| Correct Methods vs. Working Methods | 62 |
| Time Estimation Hell | 63 |

## Prematurity  67

| | |
|---|---|
| Premature Optimization | 67 |
| Premature Game Design | 69 |
| Premature Promises | 70 |
| Premature Feature Integration | 71 |
| Premature Polish | 73 |
| Stamp Design | 74 |

## Mastering Emotions  77

| | |
|---|---|
| Motivation | 78 |
| Procrastination | 82 |
| Embarrassment Happens | 83 |
| Feedback: Cure and Curse | 84 |

The First Step Is the Hardest ........................... 85
Start Somehow ............................................... 87
Price Shame .................................................... 89
Don't Take It Personally .................................. 91
Emotions Equal Sales .................................... 93

## Everyday Life Hacks ............................... 97

Knowledge Is worth Nothing ............................ 98
Discipline ......................................................... 99
Health ............................................................. 100
Speed Reading ............................................... 103
Singleton To-Do List ....................................... 106
Do First, Learn Later ...................................... 107
Expand Your Comfort Zone ............................ 108

## About the Author ..................................... 113

# Introduction

People all over the world dream about making a living from games. Designers, programmers and artists form groups and enthusiastically jump on the bandwagon to game development fame. Unfortunately many of them are not aware that cranking out design documents, code and graphics alone does not take them to the finish line. A bunch of additional project-saving skills is necessary. This is why many developers suddenly see themselves in a death march towards game development shame, where no game ever sees the day of light.

Issues like feature creep, missed deadlines, hubris and demotivation are common for inexperienced developers. Therefore they hardly ever finish their games. They may have the skills to design and implement a game. But what they are missing is the mindset to stay focused, remain on track, stay motivated and deliver in time. These are traits school hardly teaches.

This book deals with the underserved topic of how to finish a game project. Technical and artistic work are just the ingredients of the overall process. What makes them stick together and how to manage specific tasks make up the secret sauce to success.

## Motivation

This book took shape while I was struggling to finish my own games. It wasn't the code, the design or the graphics of the game which jammed the process. It simply was my mindset and the way I approached different tasks which made me fail.

I started reading books about self-management and self improvement. Additionally I started blogging about my experiences at *www.blackgolem.com*. Finally I searched for books about tricks to become a better (speak more effective) game maker who can finish his projects. To my surprise, there was no book dedicated to this specific topic. Or I just could not find them. So I took up the challenge and wrote such a book myself.

## Audience

This book is mainly written for developers, artists and executives who want to improve their method of making games. But it is useful for anybody who works project-oriented in general. Most parts of the book can be applied to non-game projects as well.

If you want to improve your entrepreneur life, boost your productivity, do more with less and have a good night sleep -

this book is for you.

## What You Will Find in This Book

When you start out making games alongside your day job, school or even as a fulltime (indie) game developer you will encounter problems you have never had before. You may think of technical difficulties like annoying bugs, how to write AI code, animating complex 3D assets or compile errors. These problems will occur. But there is a more dangerous threat out there. It's called the human factor and it makes creating games quite difficult.

This book is a set of tricks and techniques to prevent human nature from ruining your game project. Simple issues like embarrassment, procrastination or perfectionism can become death traps for your success. So you should be aware of these perils to avoid them or to cope with them.

Here are the major points discussed throughout the book:

- Going from hobby to pro game making
- Thinking no longer as an employee but as an entrepreneur
- Staying in time restraints and budget
- Improving your work habits
- Motivating yourself

This book is aimed to give you the necessary mindset to successfully design, implement and sell your games. Finally, it's your mind and willpower which make you successful. They make the difference between a thriving game studio and a bunch of hobby developers.

## What You Won't Find in This Book

Topics like game design and game technology are already discussed in other books ad nauseam. Therefore it would be a waste of time to tackle them here again. Instead I assume that you are familiar with the different disciplines of game production. You don't have to be a designer, a coder, a marketing guy and a music composer. You just should be one of them.

Here is a list of topics you won't find in here:

- Game development technology
- Game code
- Game design
- Graphics and sound
- Artificial intelligence
- Marketing and public relations
- Team management
- Game business

If you're looking for any of these topics it's time for you to close this book and head over to the *"... for Dummies"* book shelf. Acquire the single knowledge pieces of the game making puzzle there. Come back to this book when you feel overwhelmed by putting together the 1 million piece jigsaw puzzle called "my game".

## Personal Stories

Throughout the book I will share personal opinions and stories from my own game development career. They will be presented with a special formatting, like the following story:

> Once upon a time there was a little boy who made dumb table top games. After he had grown up he made less dumb digital games and wrote books.
>
> And he lived happily ever after.
>
> The End.

Most of the stories added to the wish of sharing my experiences in this book. Therefore I included them here, in the creation they have spawned.


## Gender

When it comes to writing for an unknown audience there's always the question how to handle gender. Male pronouns or female pronouns? Both? None at all? The latter is hardly feasible...

I chose the male for a simple reason: the majority of people in the games industry is male.

# Going Indie

Indie.

This word has been floating around online for over a decade now. Now is the year 2014. So many success stories fill the Internet ether, with *Braid, FTL, Super Meat Boy* and *Minecraft's* overnight success as poster children.

Reading all these impressive stories leads to a simple conclusion: making games is fun, easy and makes you rich. The first statement is true. The other two are not. At least not without good skills and luck.

But then why are so many stories about sky-rocketing indie game developers in the news? The simple answer is: this is what people want to read. Nobody wants to hear about hard work, long nights, running out of money, stressed relationships and other things you already may know from your own life. People just want the exciting stuff.

Does that mean that most indie game developers are

suffering?

No, that's not the case. But being indie is very different from being employed, regardless if it's in games or any other business. Most schools don't prepare their students for independence (in short: indie) and therefore they miss important advice how to make it as indie. School is meant to produce workers for predefined job positions[1], not independent personalities.

If you want to become a successful indie game developer you have to become a self-reliant person. This is the point where this book comes into play.

## The Dream of Overnight Success

Overnight success stories dominate the media. *Minecraft*, *Angry Birds* and *Tiny Wings* make you ponder starting your own game project. Their stories make you daydream about your own journey to fame, money and artistic expression. It just looks so easy.

There is an oft-overlooked detail though:

> *Overnight success happens after failing the foregone day and night.*

Before Markus Persson started *Minecraft* he had cut his teeth on many small, sometimes unfinished projects[2] hardly anybody knows about. *Minecraft* itself started as a rehashed version of the rather unknown game *Infiniminer*. *Rovio*, the

---

1 *www.squidoo.com/stop-stealing-dreams*
2 *www.mojang.com/notch*

studio behind *Angry Birds*, had released more than 30 "not so good" games before they rose to fame with shooting birds into pig shacks. *Tiny Wings* is an exception in this list. It took the developer about 6 months to complete the game, then it took off. Exceptions prove the rule.

There are misconceptions about how to become a successful game maker. The first one is that good games sell well by nature. When people begin making and selling things on their own they expect the world to beat a path to their doors.

Fact is: most ideas are already implemented and available on the market, in one way or another. The majority of new games is neither that innovative nor that outstanding. Why should a player buy your game instead of similar game X?

The second misconception is that a good product promotes itself. The most amazing game won't sell when nobody knows about it. Having your own website with a "buy button" on it is not enough. Driving interested people to your website is way more important. The dreaded word "marketing" comes into play.

Finally there is the hope for "getting chosen". The *App Store* is such a bottleneck, beating the drum for only a handful of lucky developers. Betting on this resembles playing the lottery for income.

Success is not the outcome of luck or help from others. The word "success" derives from "to succeed" in terms of "to result from". Success results from target-oriented dedication. Luck may make you successful for a short while. But it's the improvement of skills, the application of knowledge and plenty of trial and error that makes you successful for the long haul.

Overnight success rarely happens. It's rather that people get surprised by no-names while watching the elite.

## Screw Small Games, Mine Will Be Epic!

How do you spot a game developer who's new to the industry? He will tell you about his new game having hundreds of characters, thousands of weapons and a million hours of gameplay. The numbers are exaggerated but you get it.

Newcomers want to funnel all their dreams into one game. They don't mind that each asset and each feature takes time to implement. Therefore unrealistic ideas take shape which can't be finished in the end.

This is an important lesson to learn for indies: you can't have everything. The better rule would be: you can have only a little.

You will make plenty of mistakes in your first game. Game by game the mistakes become fewer and less critical. It's not so important to avoid mistakes. This is a myth propagated by conventional school systems. It's more important to identify mistakes, learn from them and do it better next time.

"Better next time" is a key phrase. Releasing a few small games within a year makes you a better game developer than releasing just one in the same amount of time. Lessons learned from the foregone game automatically improve the next game. Just keep in mind that your first game(s) will suck.

If you have plans for going full-time indie small projects have another advantage: they bear less risk. "All in" on one poker hand looks cool in movies but kills businesses in reality. It's better to have a few smaller chances of winning, not just one big shot.

Motivation is another factor which profits from short projects. Many games never see the light of day just because their developers suffer from fatigue. Small projects – we are speaking about a few months – are over before they get cumbersome.

A small project also need less staff. If it's small enough you even can do it on your own. No meetings, no discussions, no diverging opinions and all the income for you.

> Once I worked in a startup studio which was founded by two fresh-baked university graduates. They entered the *App Store* with the right game at the right time and took off (during the *App Store* gold rush years). They hired some people to make bigger games. Suddenly the founders found themselves no longer coding and designing games but managing their staff and having business talks. What they really wanted to do was now carried out by their employees. The staff had all the fun the founders wanted in the first place.
>
> Today they have dropped their staff and have gone back to design and code their games themselves again.

"Start small" is a universal rule. Babies crawl first, then they start walking. Weight lifters don't start out with 400 pounds. The biggest trees grow from small seeds.

Take it easy. Start small.

## Beginning, Disillusion and Transformation

When people start writing games they are enthusiastic about creating something they like with their own hands. Crazy ideas are flowing and all of them go into the game design. "It's going to be killer!"

In this phase, folks work for the joy of creation and achievement. In the beginning money is an afterthought, a by-product of the game making process, if you will. At this stage we are talking about a hobby.

While happily coding away time, raising the first playable alpha version, minor problems start to occur. Coding is fun but the issues popping up every once in a while start to get annoying. It should be fun and problem solving isn't.

After a while the first alpha version is done. But it's not as cool as expected. So much time went into the code and the assets but the visible gameplay is not what it should be. How is that possible? Aside from the scarce gameplay, hardly any of the cool ideas have been implemented yet. There is still so much work left to do.

Slowly the team becomes aware that this isn't just sunshine and roses. It smells more like work. Some team members start to lose motivation. Everything else suddenly seems more important. The dream of their own game starts to crumble and every new problem further disillusions the creators.

What now? Struggle on? Quit? Start a new game?

At this point a transformation happens. The team becomes

aware that making games isn't a cakewalk. It's work with all its ups and downs other disciplines have as well.

Some may start over now to get the good startup feeling back. Others may quit, tagging game development as "not fun", "too difficult" or "not for me". But the best teams go on and tackle the problems, one after the other. Problem solving is a basic trait for success. Rough seas make good sailors. So overcoming problems is an important skill to learn.

In later chapters this book will show you how to handle problems like disillusion, fatigue, feature creep and doubts. The key principle is prevention. Knowing how to avoid a problem is way better than knowing how to solve it. This book is a guide which will teach you how to get around the pitfalls of game development.

## Better or Different

Human beings love to categorize. People will pigeon-hole your game into a genre to make it comparable to other games. They will ask themselves: "Why should I buy this game instead of [other game of same genre]?" What will be your answer? Yours has more weapons? More characters? A lower price? More impressive graphics? Epic play length? Hats?

As you may have guessed the list goes on and on. All these answers have one thing in common: comparability. To stand out you have to have an advantage over other games in your niche. For example "greener trees" won't knock somebody's socks off. It's just too vague to be recognized as a benefit. Numbers like number of levels, number of characters or play hours are more persuasive. These numbers can be compared with the fact sheets of other titles. That's the reason why game packages sport feature bullet lists on the back. They aim for customer reactions like "wow, twice as many guns as the other game – let's buy it!"

Comparability fuels competition. Game makers producing similar games have to outperform each other to make sales. That's good for the player. Prices drop and the games get better due to forced improvement. But can you stay in business with shrinking profit margins while the pressure of "higher-faster-further" increases? Do you want that at all?

To avoid this rat race you have just one option: avoid comparability and be different.

Being different means that you should make your game as incomparable to other games as possible. This reduces competition. Less competition automatically increases your rank in a niche. Being #2 isn't that difficult when there are just two other games in your niche.

Genres don't get invented every day. So don't consider that as your goal. Just have one or two features which make your game stick out of the vast sea of "me-too" titles. Business people would call this a unique selling proposition, a USP. I call it bait to hook players and game journalists.

There's another benefit of being different: you can leave behind conventions. Genres establish rules and best practices over time. You have to either fulfill them or break them with a better solution. Either approach can be quite tough. When your game is different, it has its own rules and therefore has less conformity issues.

So what's your decision? Being better or being different?

## Choose the Right Idols

Most game developers have a favorite genre. Usually that's the genre in which they want to make games. Further developers have favorite games which they see as paragons for their own games. It's the chill going down your spine when you imagine your own version of *Assassin's Creed* or *Grand Theft Auto* in action which boosts your motivation. Well, these games are not really indie games but you get it.

Entering the ring of game development this way is romantic but also very dangerous. Replicating prominent idols has a high probability of killing your ambitions by exhausting you. The problem is that inexperienced game makers don't think about the huge amount of time, money, blood, sweat and tears which went into their paragons.

The following points highlight common pitfalls in choosing idols. Keep them in mind and save yourself from yet another never-done game project.

### *Graphics Idols*

Don't make the mistake of following eye-candy idols. Today's AAA games spend millions of dollars on visuals. As long as you can't afford an army of artists and animators you can't compete in this category. Idolizing games which have simple graphics is way easier and cheaper.

Here is a list of links to successful indie game sites which list games with simple graphics:

- *Distractionware*
- *Spiderweb Software*

- *Sword and Sworcery*
- *Towerfall Ascension*
- *Terraria*
- *Hotline Miami*
- *Super Crate Box*
- *Thomas Was Alone*
- *RYMDKAPSEL*

Even indie games climb the ladder of fancy graphics these days. Therefore "not so wealthy" game makers have to go a different route. They prefer style over realism (that is, expensiveness). The best examples for style are *Sword and Sworcery*, *Thomas Was Alone* or *RYMDKAPSEL*.

It's simple: be better or be different.

### *Multiplayer Idols*

Multiplayer games are more difficult to write than single player games. There are plenty of issues like network latency, narrow bandwidth, additional programming for servers, security holes, state persistence, load balance, etc. It's a long list of things to take care of. The complexity for testing games rises with the number of players. As you can see there are many threats which may blow your time schedule when you're not aware of them. There is also the need for knowledge and experience in network programming. I just say multi-threading.

### *Epic RPG Idols*

Are you fascinated by the epic stories of *Mass Effect, Elder Scrolls* or *Final Fantasy*? Is it your goal to provide your own role playing game with +50 hours of gameplay?

Let's take a closer look at the costs. For long hours of gameplay you will need many different types of scenery like countryside, towns, buildings, interior, temples, caves, mountains, etc. There also will be plenty of characters. At this point a costly visual style already makes it impossible for a small team to finish the project. When you have more favorable visuals there is still an epic story left to write. Depending on your writing skills it can draw a large part from your development time.

Simple graphics and 10 hours of gameplay can already ramp up to several months of work. Try measuring the time needed for creating the first few hours of your RPG and see how much time it would take to finish it. This, by the way, is a rule applicable to every game project.

## Don't Think, Do

Many people dream about following their ambitions. There are instruments they want to learn to play, books they want to write or games they want to make.

Unfortunately there is always a reason *not* to get started. Popular ones are "I'm not able to do that" or "who am I to do that" thoughts. Even when people have the knowledge and skills, they think "I'm not good enough to do that". Further reasoning: "nobody will buy this" aka "I can't charge for this". Finally the lack of spare time due to job, friends, kids or simply watching favorite TV series makes it seem like an impossible endeavor.

"I don't have any time." is a lame excuse. How much time do you spend surfing the web or watching TV? How much time are you hanging out with friends? All these activities have their value and deliver joy. Nevertheless, channeling off a few hours a week from your spare time activities won't make a big difference.

Imagine the following: you are hungry and your fridge is empty. What would you do? You would go to the next shop and buy some food. It's an everyday routine you won't think about. Now imagine this: you see a girl for the first time and you want to ask her out for a date. What would you do? (sorry ladies, I told you this book's target readership is male) Unless you're a seasoned badass, thoughts of anxiety will pop up in your mind:

- "What should I say?"
- "What if I get nervous?"
- "She is out of my league, isn't she?"
- "What if she laughs at me?"

All these thoughts bring up the worst case scenario which you finally want to avoid. It feels too dangerous to risk getting shot down in flames.

The same worst case thinking is what prevents us from doing the things we dream of. "What if they hate what I do?". It's the fear of failure which holds us back. The first example of buying food does not bear this threat. You already know that there's nothing to fear. The latter example of approach anxiety resembles the fear of failure you may have when thinking about doing something new like writing a game. People may not like your attempt. So you don't even try.

Now you may think "What are you talking about? I'm already coding my game and it's nearly finished". Well, are you already selling it for real cash? Making a game resembles pondering how to approach the girl. Selling it is the step where you walk over to her and open your mouth. Player feedback resembles the answer she gives you. The feedback is what you fear.

OK, now that we know the problem - what's the solution?

Using the girl approach metaphor, it's much easier to approach a girl you're not interested in. Ask her the time, ask for a light or just give her a smile while walking by. Next time bandy a few words. Following this metaphor, keep your first game simple, don't expect anything and see what the resonance is. Learn from that and try again with a more extensive game. Rinse, repeat. Don't worry about your reputation. As long as you keep it honest and friendly, nothing can go wrong.

Soon you will have the knowledge and guts to accomplish and sell the games you really want to make. This is the moment when you stop dissuading yourself from doing it and get started. It's easy now because you know there is no real danger except in your own mind.

The same goes for the ladies.

---

I always wanted to write a book. I started a novel at the age of 16 but never finished it. Nobody ever read these

> 150 pages because I feared getting laughed at.
>
> Fast forward to 2012: I was coding a game and listened to *Rage Against the Machine*. Then my thoughts strayed off to book writing. I had a few ideas for books but still hesitated. Then I heard the *Guerrilla Radio* lyrics:
>
> *What better place than here, what better time than now?*
>
> I stopped coding and started writing my first book about collision detection[3].
>
> Sometimes you just need a sign.

## The Nay-Sayers

Everything that's beyond common sense is hard to accept for most people. When there is something revolutionary on the horizon, they try to approve it with common sense. The problem with revolutions is: they change common sense. Therefore they often get declined because they look odd or threaten the status quo.

Love has to be a roller-coaster of emotions, devotion till death, roses all over the bed, Mr. and Mrs. Right, etc. This is what television and movies show us all day long. But our gut feeling tells us that there is more to it. There are many more possibilities to keep a fulfilling relationship.

---

[3] *www.collisiondetection2d.net*

The same holds true for games. Does a platformer game always have to have the possibility of jumping? What about elevators? What about teleportation or a grappling hook?

When you come up with an odd game idea, many will say "that won't work". First of all: do they have the background in game development to tell you so? And if they have, what is the reasoning behind their opinion? How can they predict the future of your idea? Nobody knows the future. Thus, nobody can know if your idea will soar or bomb until you have proved one of the two.

Derek Sivers, the founder of *CDBaby*, said:

> *"Revolution is a word that people use when you are successful. Before that, you are just a corky person who does things differently."*

Evolution extends common sense gently. Revolution, on the other hand, jumps at the uncommon sense and transforms it into common sense. Therefore, if you have no nay-sayers against you, you hardly can have a revolutionary idea. Right?

# From Slave to Master

Children, students and employees have something in common: they have authorities that tell them what to do. On the one hand, this is really annoying. Sometimes you just don't feel like doing what your parents, teacher or boss wants you to do. On the other hand, it frees you from decisions and responsibility. When your boss tells you to work on a new task, you don't have to think about if this task is worth the effort. That's your boss' problem.

When you become self-employed, some kind of schizophrenia will (have to) emerge in your mind. You will become a master-slave hybrid. As the slave you have to design the game, write the code, do the audio, test the game, and so on. As the master you have to make market-driven decisions, cut features and force your slave-self to work extra hours. This is especially the case for solo indies. If you work with other people you still will have to wear more than one hat. One day you craft something just to decide to throw it away the very next day.

Usually compromises are made between 2 or more people. Self-employed entrepreneurs have to make compromises between their personalities.

A big threat of being your own boss is the freedom to take time off whenever you want. When you are part-time indie that's not as dangerous as when you're full-time indie. If you have a day job, skipping your spare time project does not affect your income. At least not immediately. Full-time indies who skip work also skip progress and therefore stop money from coming in.

The following chapters will show you tricks and insights how to make the transition from employee to self-employee.

## You Get Paid per Sale, Not per Hour

As an employee you receive your pay checks on a regular basis. What you do and how well you do it has no direct effect on your money stream. Self-employment, on the other hand, means you don't get any money for making a game. You only get money when you sell it. So it's no longer your goal to fill your day with working hours. Now it's your job to score as many sales as possible. Don't get me wrong - it's not just about marketing. A good game is mandatory. But marketing is what makes your game visible to potential customers.

Try to keep a work journal for a little while and enter all your working hours in it. Then multiply the number of hours with the hourly wage you want. The result - how fast money goes down the drain - may be surprising.

When you keep in mind that everything you do has to pay itself off in some way, you start to think like a business man. You will start looking for ways to cut down your work, optimize tasks, reuse code and use third-party software more often. You will consider buying commercial tools, paying for services and buying assets instead of doing everything yourself. For example, searching for a free texture, coloring it, fixing repetitive patterns and making it seamless is often more expensive than buying a canned texture for a few bucks online. When you start out without a budget, doing it yourself is OK. But as soon as you have money at hand, rethinking the best economical option becomes important.

## Have Goals

Many game developers start their career as a hobby. They write games for the sake of it, because it's what they like to do. As long as the work itself brings joy there is no need for a goal. But as soon as they want to make a living from their hobby, new priorities take shape. The main priority is, as you may guess, making enough money to stay in business. Despite the fact that this is obvious, newbie indies keep doing what they did as a hobby: having limitless fun. The fun keeps being unbound until the money is depleted.

> I was once one of these easygoing indies. Bankruptcy is not the end of the world but it cures naivety the hard way.

Goals have an uncomfortable trait: not meeting them is

failure. Maybe that's the reason why people avoid having goals or pursuing them. Who wants to set up his own emotional punishment anyway?

But why are goals missed? One explanation for this is the wrong scope. "I want to make a living from games" is way too vast a resolution. On the other hand, "I want to make $1 from my game" sounds too simple to be a serious goal. But why not? It sounds achievable. The game does not have to be clever, beautiful or epic. It just has to earn you a single buck.

A narrow scope is what bootstraps success and the accompanying feeling of confidence. Start with a small goal, reach it, feel good and set up the next one. Raise the bar as you go along. Break down goals into subgoals when they get too big. Flesh out an action plan for each goal to know what needs to be done. It's easy to get lost in game development without a roadmap.

Some plans will work out, others won't. Find out what does not work and use this knowledge for further planning. This is important especially for time estimation. When goals and deadlines keep being unmet, plans become pointless.

The skill of setting and achieving goals is an important characteristic of successful people. Money is just a side effect of success. It *succeeds* from being an achiever.

## Focus

Employment usually means working in a specific domain. Programming, 2D graphics, 3D modeling, audio, testing, management, public relations, you name it.

When you become self-employed this belongs to the past. You will have to wear several hats. Let's say you're a coder with an artist to help you out. This means you have the following jobs (at least):

- CEO
- Lead programmer
- Lead tester
- Public relations
- Coffee machine expert

Simply put, you have to do everything yourself. Does this mean you have to do everything simultaneously?

You may have heard of multitasking. It's the art of doing different things at the same time. This is a business owner's wet dream. One worker who can do several jobs at once. No extra ancillary wage costs. That would be great!

Forget about multitasking, it's a misconception. It's true that human beings can do several tasks at once, for example walking while eating while talking on their mobile phone. This is possible because walking and eating don't need much conscious brain power. Multitasking has its limits when it comes to full-focus tasks like writing source code while talking to somebody. It simply does not work.

> When I'm driving and talking to my co-driver, my brain immediately switches to autopilot mode. This means I either drive home or hit the road towards the town where I'm currently living in.

> Sometimes I'm not aware of the wrong direction until my co-driver asks me where I'm heading to.
>
> No joke.

The solution for handling multiple tasks in parallel can be learned from central processor unit cores (CPUC) in computers. A CPUC runs one execution thread at a time. When a CPUC has to execute multiple threads simultaneously it uses context switching. This means it runs one thread for a short time, switches over to the next, runs this thread for a short time, switches to the next, and so on. CPUCs focus on one task at a time and switch over in a scheduled manner.

The conclusion is simple: focus on one task at a time.

Aside from the clear separation of different tasks, there is also the alignment of tasks to your brain capacities. Writing code, for example, needs a different type of brain power than answering emails. Animating 3D models needs other brain areas than designing levels does. Some tasks can be carried out better in the morning while others fit better in the afternoon or at night. This is different for every person. So find out what works best for you and schedule your work accordingly.

Last but not least: forget ordinary working hours. If you are fully motivated on weekends, work on weekends. If your best time is 4am than get started at 4am. If you love to work at night get some coffee and burn the midnight oil. I'm aware this can heavily interfere with a day job, family and friends.

Nevertheless, it's worth being taken into consideration. It's better to work highly focused for two hours at 4am than wasting the same hours at 6pm when you're tired from your day job.

## Reduce Context Switching

This chapter goes hand in hand with the chapter Focus. The chapter Focus suggests that context switching is a good thing. It is. Nonetheless, it follows the common rule *less is more*. With context-switching comes switch overhead. When you switch to another task, it takes time to pause the current task and get into the new one. Then, after working on the second task for a while, you have the overhead of going back to the first task. The overhead of this context-switching can be quite high. It can go as far as to ruin your motivation for the whole day.

When you keep the switching frequency as low as possible, you foster "the flow". This is the state of mind which makes you 100% focused on your current work. Everything comes naturally in this state. People get lost in the flow for several hours, just to get brought back by their growling bellies. It's common to forget about time, space and food intake if you are in "the flow". It's the synchronicity of your vibe and the vibe of your work which makes you become one with it.

Distractions like meetings or small side jobs (or even day jobs) are often inevitable. The trick is to block them together in as few interruptions as possible. This is the same reason why some offices have limited hours open to the public. It's simply a reduction to one context switch a day, from serving citizens to working through piled up work.

Be into a task when you call it a day. This is a simple ruse to get back into the task faster when you take it up the next day. The psychological background is that a small sub-task is easier to continue than tackling a whole new task. The smaller the mental image of the task in your mind, the faster you can gain momentum.

## Keep a Work Journal

Employers want to know how much time their employees spend on their tasks. First and foremost, this is for comparing the timetable with the real numbers. If there's too much overtime a red light starts flashing at the boss' desk. Understandably, the project falls behind schedule with each extra hour.

Having an eye on your own progress is also important when you are self-employed. Any schedule is useless when its tasks always take longer than planned. To know if you're behind schedule, you have to take notes about your work hours.

A simple spread sheet as a work journal is enough. This work trace should enable you to get an overview of how much time went into which part of your project.

> My own work journal is a simple OpenOffice spreadsheet with the columns *date, work description, duration* and *work category*. The category column contains only a few different values like *"gfx creation"*, *"coding"* or *"design"*. This simple setup lets me generate nice pie charts from the time and category

> columns which tell me how long I spend on which category.

That's all very well, but what are these statistics good for?

First of all, it tells you what your hourly wage is. Take the project's generated income and divide it by the sum of its work hours. Often this makes one thing clear: you would earn more if you went back to the treadmill of employment. Another insight is that more work for the same income thins out your hourly wage. Therefore, future work has to be more effective regarding income generation than finished work. This is especially true for marketing.

Secondly, a work journal allows you to derive estimations from former tasks, for example, from creating a mid-sized enemy unit. You can't say two similar tasks will take the same time. But you can assume that the upcoming task will take plus/minus a few hours or days of what the last similar task took. That's a lot better than a shot in the dark.

Thirdly, a proper journal and its statistics can tell you where you should start optimizing your performance. If the graphics take up half of your budget, it would be wise using a simpler graphics style, get faster at cranking out assets or hiring a more efficient artist.

> After completing the first endboss for my shoot 'em up game *Nordenfelt*, I analyzed the work hours for this task. The coding hours took up more than 40%. A little detail research in the work journal made it clear: it's the test-

> adapt-test cycle in combination with recompilation. To speed this up, I integrated a script language. No longer having to recompile C++ code gave the cycle a higher momentum.

Last but not least, knowing how long your project took is great for your next game. If your last game is well-received, you may consider a successor. The good thing about successors is that the code base is already there. So you can estimate that coding will take up less time than it did for the first game. This way, it's easier to set a release date for the second installment.

## Restrict Yourself

Modern computers are so powerful, you can implement nearly anything you want for them. Photo-realism, for example, wasn't possible on the old consoles and computers of the 90s. Today it is. Modern technology creates a vacuum of endless possibilities which is tempting to fill. The sky is the limit. The only restriction is your budget. There are so many opportunities, but so little time and money.

Self-imposed restrictions are your best friend in this regard. Limit yourself for the sake of completing your game. Cut down the screen resolution and reduce the color palette. Avoid physics engines and abstract your animations. Limit controls to the D-pad and one button. You can surely come up with more constraints for your own game.

That sounds like handicapping yourself. Why should you do

that?

Many amazing things result from restrictions and scarcity. There are several proverbs which apply here:

> *Necessity begets ingenuity.*

> *Less is more.*

> *However large the ear, it cannot hear seven speeches at once.*

> *Perfection is achieved when there is nothing left to take away.*

> *You can often find in rivers what you cannot find in oceans.*

Sometimes, sticking to your self-imposed restrictions can be hard. For example, when you want to add a new specific particle effect to your engine which it does not support yet. This is when the feature creep starts.

---

Once I started coding a game called *Amorphous* (it's a bad sign if you have a name for your product before it is definite - true for books and *Amorphous*). It was a strategy game heavily influenced by *X-Com* and *Silent Storm*. It had large maps and a rectangular floor raster similar to the *X-Com* games. When I saw the first melee fight of two units in *Amorphous* I became aware that they needed to stand closer together during the battle. Therefore I increased the resolution of the floor raster. This way the unit movement became smoother and melee fights could be fought at the right distance.

Unfortunately, this caused some problems. The high-resolution raster made the path-finding algorithm halt the game for a few seconds each time I commanded a unit to go somewhere far off. Back then I didn't know anything about hierarchical path search or navigation meshes. So it was an insurmountable obstacle for me. Further, the memory consumption of the raster cells exploded. If my memory serves me right, it was about 50MB per floor, with 5 possible floors per level. Don't ask me what was stored in these cells. Most of it was just over-the-top realism crap like clearance height for different unit sizes.

Today I would stick to the low-resolution floor raster. It does not matter if units really can reach each other with their melee weapons. It just has to serve the gameplay which does not need realism of this kind. Most games are abstract anyway. So there is no need for realistic combats when everything else is actually symbolic.

Limiting movement and animations to an abstract level would have saved me tons of development time. At least it made for a nice anecdote about my greenhorn game

> dev years.

Work with what you already have. If a new feature can't be implemented with your engine's current feature set, reconsider whether you really need the new feature. Keep in mind that each extension has to be designed, implemented and tested. Is the new feature worth it?

An interesting side effect of restrictions, hardware-dependent or artificial, is that they define stereotypes. Mario's moustache and blue overalls, for example, are results from low screen resolution for the Donkey Kong arcade machines. Sprite art would not exist if old computers provided more than just a handful of colors per sprite. Isometric-view games would not have become that stereotypical if this form of pseudo-3D wouldn't have been so easy to implement and resource-efficient for the 2D machines of the 80s and 90s.

Sometimes restrictions can get in your way. But then, they avert feature creep, keep you focused on the important things like gameplay, force ingenuity and keep your code simple.

Limits simply work.

## Seek & Destroy Bottlenecks

The same way you fix frame rate drops in a game, you should fix bottlenecks in your work process. There are always steps which need much time. Usually these are manual tasks like bundling your game and its assets into a zip file. Uploading this bundle is another task, often done by hand.

When you find yourself repeating a specific task often, try to write a script which does the work for you. This can be a simple *Windows batch* script or something more sophisticated like *Python* or *JavaScript*. Software test suites, build steps, asset filters and deploys are predestined for scripting. Build server software already covers many of these aspects. Yet there are tasks which should run just locally, for example wiping out temporary files of some kind. Keep automation in mind and you will find plenty of possibilities to boost your daily work.

Another bottleneck destroyer is extruding game settings and often-changed functionality into configuration files and scripts. I would suggest scripts also for settings. They can be used as configuration files as well as for defining behaviour. Recompilation needs much time. Scripts don't need recompilation. Without the need for a compiler, in combination with access to a game's assets, the game also becomes moddable. This can be a big advantage when you want to build an active community around your game.

Keep in mind that languages and their environments have different attributes. If you write your whole game in a script language like *Python*, for example, then there is no reason to include configuration files. You can define your settings in *Python* scripts anyway. On the other hand, if you write your game in a compiled language like *C++*, configuration files and scripts will increase your work performance a lot.

Aside from the technical bottlenecks, there may be a mental bottleneck: low concentration. Forcing yourself to work when you have no concentration left is counterproductive. Your effectiveness will approach level zero mercilessly. It would be just a waste of time. Instead refill your concentration tank with a simple trick: rest. Either for 10 minutes or for 10 hours if you need. But rest when your mind gets weary.

## The Curse of Do It Yourself

Coders love to have control over as many parts of their software as possible. This easily leads to a do-everything-yourself attitude. It feels great to write code which stretches from the GUI to the metal and does exactly what you want it to do. It feels like dominating the machine and tickles the god complex in us.

A good programmer writes quality code in decent time. A better coder builds software from preexisting parts in less time. The former is the mason, the latter is the architect. Guess who gets more money and kudos.

Carl Sagan, astronomer and author of the novel *Contact*, once said:

> *"If you wish to make an apple pie from scratch, you must first invent the universe."*

This quote makes it clear that "from scratch" isn't possible. There is always a raised level zero, a set of existing parts and tools to start with. Even if you write everything yourself, you have to use at least a text editor and a compiler. So why not use as much $3^{rd}$ party software as possible to get faster and cheaper results? If you really want to learn the basics of game engines, write an engine. But if you want to make a game, be sure to cover as much functionality as possible with available software. This frees up your time for the game-defining parts which you have to implement anyway.

There are plenty of libraries, tools and middleware out there for free. But be aware that free software often does not get the same care as paid software. There are many factors beside the price to consider when you are searching for $3^{rd}$ party software:

- License
- Features
- Age
- Extensibility
- Support
- Community
- Simplicity
- Documentation

Tools which cost less than $100 amortize very fast. Always ask yourself - how many of your working hours are equivalent to the price? How long would it take to code it yourself? Self-made libraries, engines and tools need lots of care. Care equals working hours. Working hours equals cash. Can you afford to do it yourself?

## Getting Better by Intention

With practice, you get better at anything you do. Steady programming, for example, makes you code faster and think more logically. Getting better at your daily business is natural. Nevertheless, this natural progress often just takes you to the local maximum. The term "local maximum" comes from mathematics and means "the maximum within a specific range". In the case of natural progress (of any discipline), the range is called our comfort zone. Athletes, for instance, always go beyond their comfort zones. Growth happens outside your current limits. Athletes check out how other athletes perform and train to get better than them. In mathematical terminology, this would be going for the global maximum aka the best anyone can perform in this sport.

Now I don't want you or your team to compete with all the big and successful game development studios out there. I just want you to go beyond your own limitations. Let's say you took the time for drawing animation cycles for character sprites. One animation cycle takes you about 2 hours. Could you do it within 1 hour? Or even within half an hour? Usually faster drawing won't get you there. It's more about streamlining your work, learning to be less precise (big one) and designing (that is to say, deciding) before you flesh out the details. The hour limit or half-hour limit may not be possible. Nevertheless, the attempt of tackling these limits takes you out of your local maximum to your own global maximum.

A further trick for pushing your maxima is to read a lot. Read news about game development, blogs, books, magazines - whatever serves you. Read regularly. Set yourself a minimum of books you want to read in a year, for example 1 book per month. As long as you keep your knowledge at its current level, you can optimize your effectiveness and efficiency just to the boundaries of this knowledge level. Apply your knowledge continuously so that it manifests in your daily deeds. Knowledge without application is worth nothing.

Aside from the advantageous challenges it's beneficial to

experiment with new tools, procedures and disciplines. Have an experiment per week, per month or whatever interval you are comfortable with. Set aside time for exploring new territories.

> My calendar reminds me once a month to spare one day for an experiment. I have a list of experiment ideas, going from "try script language X" over "compose a song" to "invest in stocks".
>
> When this reminder pops up, I always think "I don't have the time right now". But then, I think about the percentage one day is in a month. It's less than 5%. If I can't spare these few hours, I'm doing something wrong.
>
> Experiments bring different results. One non-starter was the attempt to sell digital assets on stock sites. Another, more successful, was trying the *Squirrel* script language. It's so much easier now to test AI than it was with pure C++. Long compilation times are very distracting.

Another way to get faster is doing less. Cut off unnecessary work like pointless meetings, reading irrelevant blogs or discussing in forums just for the sake of it. Resist the temptation of polish when it's not necessary. Don't add game engine features which you don't really need.

## Security

Have you ever heard your computer beep suddenly, followed

by a virus warning popping up on your screen and watched this virus delete your game project from your hard drive immediately? Even if this horror scenario is rather improbable, it can happen anytime. It does not have to be a virus. It simply can be your laptop getting out of hand, crashing on the floor and ruining your hard drive, undoing months or years of hard work.

> Once, my girlfriend at that time was playing games on my laptop while I was at work. When I came home, she was all in tears. She had spilled a glass of juice all over my laptop keyboard. Accidentally, of course. A cold shiver ran down my spine. My whole (now defunct) project had been on that laptop. I hadn't made regular backups back then, just occasional snapshots of the project folder, stored on a rewritable CD. What if everything was lost?
>
> Despite the total loss of the laptop, I was able to save all the important data on an external hard drive. This incident taught me two lessons: backup regularly and keep liquids away from the machine.

Regular backups should not be neglected. They can be as simple as copying snapshots of your project to an external hard drive. Set yourself a reminder to do so. Better yet, automate the backup via a scheduled script or a dedicated backup tool. Everything that runs automatically is good.

Backups should be stored on a medium physically separated from your workstation. For example, integrate a hard drive for backups into your LAN. You can also use *Dropbox*, *Google Drive* or similar services to store your backups online. Every service that synchronizes backup folders automatically is welcome.

A more sophisticated solution would be a version control system like *Git, Mercurial* or *SVN*. Either you run them on your own server, hard drive or you use one of the many online version control services like Assembla, GitHub or Bitbucket.

> I use a heterogeneous backup environment. Firstly, I have a *SVN* repository, mainly for projects including coding and writing. Not all project files go into this repository, e.g. drafts and temporary files. Therefore, I clone my whole hard drive every two weeks and store the image on an external hard drive. Active projects reside in a *Dropbox* folder. This way I can access them from multiple devices and can restore their latest versions with all unversioned files (regarding *SVN*) without consulting the latest image on the external backup hard drive.

Last but not least, there are viruses, worms and similar threatening pieces of sh..., ahem, software, lurking in the shadows of the internet. Using a simple, free virus scanner is better than not using any protection at all.

And please, for god's sake, keep drinks away from your machine.

# Agility

Old school software development was done, and sometimes still gets done, like building a house: design it, draw the plan and build it. This methodology sounds appropriate but has a fundamental flaw. Software, in contrast to a house, has many novel parts. So there are unknown details which unfold their complexity only while the project is already in progress. This dynamic makes it hard to estimate the costs upfront.

Agile software development (ASD) tackles the problem of unknown details in new software. ASD is an umbrella term for different methodologies like *Scrum, Extreme Programming* or *Feature-Driven Development* which can be combined. I won't go into detail about ASD here. I just want to put it in a nutshell:

> *ASD is software development in small, efficient steps, directed by user feedback.*

Imagine it like driving a car along an unknown road. You know that the road leads to the goal but not how its course will unfold. With a car, you won't set course towards your goal and start driving as the crow flies. This works for planes or ships in open water. Cars, on the contrary, would immediately crash into the next building or would fall down a cliff. Driving a car needs continuous direction adjustment to follow the course of the road.

Using the car-driving metaphor for ASD, you regularly have to check where the road leads (user feedback) and where to turn the steering wheel next (adapting plans). This way you can navigate around all the unknown obstacles and roadblocks to reach your goal.

ASD allows you to adapt plans according to emerging information. Think, for example, about a game which allows the player to ride on arbitrary animals. In theory, it sounds amazing to cross the land on a horse, a bear or even a dragon. But testing this feature in the game made it clear that riding players have such high advantages in speed and combat over walking players, it ruins the whole gameplay. This became clear *after* the feature had been implemented. Now either countermeasures in game design can be taken to balance the gameplay or the riding feature has to be removed completely. Without ASD, you would be doomed to keep it in the game as it was planned.

## Scrum 101

*Scrum* is a light-weight ASD methodology, used by many companies all over the world. The tag "light-weight" means that this methodology introduces only a small management overhead to a project. *Scrum* is easy to learn and, in contrast to old project management methodologies, is simple to maintain. It does not stand in the way of developers but focuses their efforts on the goal.

### *An Introduction to Scrum*

Software projects usually have a financier, somebody who pays for the project and its results. In *Scrum* this person is called the *product owner*. Usually this is a customer. For indie teams, this is the team itself. Otherwise the venture wouldn't be ind(-i-)e(-pendent). The product owner creates a prioritized wish list called a *product backlog*. Indie teams form their product backlog in game design discussions. It's good to have a moderator for these discussions, called *Scrum master*. Typically this is the team leader. Somebody has to have the final world.

Work is separated into *sprints* which usually last two to four weeks. When a new sprint starts, the team pulls a small chunk from the top of the product backlog, a sprint backlog, and decides how to implement those pieces.

The team members meet each day to share their progress. There are three basic questions which have to be answered by everybody:

- What did I do yesterday?
- What will I do today?
- Is there any problem which needs to be solved?

This way the *Scrum* master gets an overview, what the current state of progress is. Furthermore, it's good for the whole team to know what the allies are working on right now.

Progress-halting problems are detected early and can be wiped out before they get a chance to stall the whole project.

At the end of a sprint, the work should be shippable. In game development, this means either a game prototype, an alpha or beta version, the final version or a patch for the released game. Normally shipping means just uploading the newest version to a server or portal, accompanied by a release note via email or blog post.

After shipping the latest version, the team reviews the sprint and decides what can be improved for the next one. There could be tasks which were too large for the last sprint or a lack of tools which kept productivity low. The former gets noticed if people are working on one task for several days in a row. Try to break down big task into smaller, one-day accomplishments.

The product owner checks out the latest version and updates the product backlog. In game development this is done by the whole team, influenced by player feedback.

As the next sprint begins, the team fetches another chunk from the product backlog and starts the sprint. This is when the cycle starts over.

*Scrum* is a time-boxed method to develop software incrementally. Development happens in self-contained steps, the sprints, where external influence is not allowed. Feedback and adjustment is only allowed between sprints. Because there should be a shippable product after each sprint *Scrum* forces early playable game versions naturally. So it saves you from procrastinating releases. What's done gets issued.

## Accept Imperfection

The very first thing you have to internalize for ASD is the fact that nothing is perfect. But hardly any software exists which is entirely bug-free. But your job is not writing bug-free code or drawing perfect sprites anyway. Your job is to get as close to perfect as possible with an adequate amount of effort.

Get used to imperfection. For example, your main character's hair may have small clipping errors (hair goes into body). Hardly any player would complain about that. So why fix it? A counterexample would be slightly odd collision detection. This can kill your gameplay immediately. That's something you should fix as soon as possible. Different flaws have different severities. Don't worry about every little bug or flaw that pops up. Note all issues in an issue list and forget them for the moment. Come back to the list when your current task is done. Find the most critical issues and fix them. Some may be left unchanged when time runs out. Nobody will care because the issues leftover are the least significant ones.

Most products are not perfect. Their creators know that but the customers don't. They just assume it. Therefore always ask yourself if a specific issue will be noticed by anybody other than you. If so, is it really crucial? Only if you can answer both questions with "yes" - should the issue be fixed.

## The Pareto Principle

The *Pareto principle*, better known as the *80-20 rule*, says that 80% of the effects come from 20% of the causes. It can also be interpreted as 20% of the inputs create 80% of the outputs. Here are some examples to illustrate what this means:

- 80% of gameplay is executed by 20% of the code.
- 20% of the customers generate 80% of the income.
- 80% of complaints come from 20% of the users.

There are also variations of this rule, like 90-10, 95-5 or 99-1. However, they all state that a fraction of the overall effort brings most of the results.

Tim Ferriss recommends in his bestseller *The 4-Hourweek* focusing on the most important 20% and skipping the other 80%. Additionally, he gives the advice to get rid of the 20% which cause 80% of the hassle you have.

Now, how does this rule apply to game development? If you think about the core mechanics of your game, you will realize, that they resemble 20% of your work which drive 80% of the fun. The rest is decoration aka graphics, audio, gameplay depth, optional features, etc. On a lower level, e.g. asset creation, you can also find that the bigger part of many assets is done in a fraction of their amount of work. What makes it take so long are the details. On a higher level, you can check out which games of your portfolio make the most income. If the support for a less lucrative game becomes a nuisance, stop supporting it. If your game needs deploy systems for several platforms like PC, Mac, Android or iOS, you can cut off the peanut-generating platforms. Always compare what the cost is and what the gain is.

The *80-20 rule* also is good for time estimation. When you think most of your work is done (that is to say, 80%), you still need four times more work to get to the finish line. This disproportionality makes it clear why many projects fall behind schedule.

## Parkinson's Law

*Parkinson's Law* says that work expands so as to fill the time available for its completion. This means, if you schedule one year for a game, for example, it will take one year to complete it. If you budget only six months, it will magically be done within this shorter time span.

Why is this? And how short can a schedule get?

*Parkinson's Law* does not say anything about the outcome. Depending on how much you shrink your time frame by, quality and scope will get reduced. This does not have to be proportional, though. Reducing a one-year plan to a period of 6 months may not compromise your game's quality. But cutting it back to a quarter, the number of features and hours for polish will have to shrink.

This can be explained with the *80-20 rule*. Let's assume we have a game project schedule spanning over 100 days. The core gameplay takes 20% of the time, which is 20 days. Now we have 80 days left for to add new features like enemy variety, more locations, a score board, etc. Further, let's say we get one feature done in 10 days which results in 8 additional features. When we cut back the project schedule to only 50 days, we get only 3 features done. This may be enough when the less important features get skipped. Now, what happens when we go even more tight, for example 30 days? Then we can implement only the most important feature. This scope may be not sufficient for players to pick up your game. So there is a minimum for how short schedules can be.

Another explanation for the time indifference is that people work more efficiently when they are under pressure. If there is plenty of time left, people take it easy. But if a deadline appears on the horizon, they gain momentum. A shorter schedule casts more light on the release date. Therefore, people will be more focused on the important work and won't get lost in details.

*Parkinson's Law,* in combination with the *80-20 rule* can reduce your work tremendously. They are also very helpful in focusing your efforts on the important work. They just demand the guts to cut back gameplay depth, features, game length, graphics, bug fixes and polish. But this is an emotional skill you have to develop anyway, if you want to work in an agile way.

## Get Yourself an Agile Mindset

One of my major problems in the past was being late. I was unable to get anywhere on time. There was always something I started just before I had to go to meet a date. There always was this gut feeling which told me that "this short task can be done in a minute". My gut feeling turned out to be the worst time estimator ever.

Now I no longer trust this feeling. I use task lists instead.

When I have an appointment with a client, for example, I set up a simple list like this:

- Prepare the prototype

- Make a presentation
- Have a meal

The list is sorted by importance. Thus the most important task is the prototype. Without it, it would not make sense to meet the client. After the top task is done the next one gets tackled. This is repeated until everything is done or I have to hit the road. The worst case would be when the prototype takes up all the time and I have to show up at the customer's place without the presentation and I'm a little hungry.

This example should illustrate the following points:

- Do the most important thing first.
- Skip tasks you can't complete, whatever it is.
- An agile mindset helps in projects as well as in everyday life.

You may get tempted to rearrange a task list while you are cleaning it. Don't give in to this gut feeling. You, or more precisely, your boss-self, have/has set the order according to rational reasoning. So the priorities are defined and you have to comply with them.

ASD relies on adaption which relies on optional tasks. The smaller and the more there are of them, the more flexible your project becomes. Start to think in terms like *prioritized, optional* and *minimal*. Set priorities and start with the most important task, not with the first in line. Keep tasks as small as possible. Drop incomplete stuff when time runs out. Cut everything that doesn't fit in, even if it's a favorite of yours. Update priorities regularly or according to new circumstances.

This way the agile mindset will soon sneak into your project management skills. Sometimes you will revert to old behavioral patterns, for example working overtime to add a new feature at the last moment. Changing a mindset is continuous work, so don't get deterred if you fail sometimes.

> I am still late sometimes. But sometimes is better than always.

## Start Lean

Software companies often have sophisticated infrastructures. This includes large and bright office rooms, top-notch hardware, multiple high resolution monitors per desk, server rooms, build servers, issue tracking software, version control systems, dedicated homepages, *Facebook* pages, *Twitter* accounts and so on and so forth. It's tempting to get such an infrastructure for your own start-up. It has this professional appeal and seems to be common courtesy for software development of today.

Now ask yourself: What do you and your team *really* need to accomplish your goals? Do you need the latest hardware? Self-hosted servers which run your issue tracker and version control system? A *Facebook* page? What about a dedicated office? An office is mandatory, isn't it?

The question is not what today's standard equipment is but what *your minimum requirements* are. The very first thing you will need is a PC or Mac. It can be a laptop or a desktop machine. It should be stronger than your game's minimum requirements. The second important part is an Internet connection. You could go without one but it's way easier and faster to solve problems with online help. Furthermore, it becomes helpful when you want to acquire middleware and do your marketing.

> Outlining the Internet as an optional tool feels a little sarcastic.

The last thing you need is your game-making skills.

That's it.

At the beginning you don't need your own website, a *Facebook* page, a build server or an issue tracking system. Set them up when the time has come for them. Keep them out as long as there is no need for them. Don't use tools just for the sake of it. This may sound self-evident but fancy "gadgets" promise the feeling of sophistication. Who doesn't want to seem professional?

Keep your infrastructure, that is, hardware and software, as lean as possible. Start with simple tools. Here are some examples of light-weight solutions anybody can use for free:

- Spread sheets for work journals, calculations and evaluations
- *Google Docs* for collaboration
- *Dropbox* and/or zip archives for backup systems
- Simple .txt files for to-do lists

Your toolbox should grow along with your needs instead of

you adapting to a bloated infrastructure. Switch to better tools on demand, not because they make you feel more professional.

## Plans Are Worthless, Planning Is Everything

The title of this chapter is a quote which was coined by Dwight D. Eisenhower, the 34th president of the United States.

At first glance it does not make any sense. Planning is done to make plans which are worthless in the end? Why should we plan at all then?

This quote embodies the essence of ASD. You always have to plan your next steps while being aware that they can change any time. Eisenhower's quote means that it's vital to keep figuring out what to do next. Revisit your plans on a regular basis and adapt them to the current circumstances.

Despite the volatility of short-term plans, it's important to have a fixed overall strategy. It defines the rough steps to your goal. These steps will then become more detailed as you address them.

## Software Is Organic

When I graduated from university, my understanding of writing software was of sequential nature: design it, build it, test and release it. We ran all our exercise projects this way.

> ASD was a fairly new concept back then. That may have

> been the reason why I had this outdated view on software project management.

Out in the field of employment I became aware that:

- Software is never "final".
- Software is an invisible art.
- Adapting code is the rule, not the exception.

There is no limit how many features software, of any kind, can have. You can always add one more. Therefore there is no such thing as a final state. You just work until you can release version 1.0. Software gets abandoned, not finished.

Does the question "When will it be finished?" sound familiar to you? Have you ever answered your project leader with the words "That's hard to tell." or "It depends." because you hadn't anything to show, even after several weeks of work? Inexperienced programmers tend to think of software as homogenous constructions. It's either done or it's not. That's true if you build it bottom-up, layer by layer. This way the visible part (mainly the user interface) is always the last step. Logically, your work won't be visible until the end. There is a solution to this problem: take a single feature of the software and fully implement it. Then do the next feature. If a feature is too big, break it up into smaller features if possible. This way software can grow in small, visible steps. Demonstrating progress becomes easy. Furthermore, your motivation will remain at a high level fueled by the small accomplishments.

Last but not least there is adaptation. Imagine a building under construction. The owner inspects the construction site but isn't happy about the results. His complaints are "I would prefer this ceiling to be higher" and "the baths should be on the other side of the building". Such changes would be very expensive and would blow the completion date. So changing the construction plan is not an option.

Software, on the other hand, is highly adaptable. It's much easier and cheaper to "raise the ceiling" and "move the baths" in software than in architecture. There is no material involved, just working hours. Good software design makes changes cheaper. If you're using a version control system like *Git, Mercurial* or *SVN* you can even restore an old version of your software in a breath. In contrast: restoring an old version of a building would be very expensive.

The statement is clear. Software grows and changes as long as you work on it. It's vital to extend and adapt it in small, iterative steps. Prepare your mind and projects for these principles and your productivity and motivation will get a boost.

## Correct Methods vs. Working Methods

In school, everything is about correct answers, correct results, correct techniques and correct behaviour. As opposed to this, real life does not care about correctness. The only question which matters is: does it work?

Money counting machines in banks are an interesting example regarding correct vs. working. When you throw a handful of coins into such a machine you would not notice a few percent incorrectness. You would have to count the coins beforehand to find out if it works correctly. This would make a mockery of using the machine. Correctness may not be given but it works in the eye of the beholder.

The money counting machine example stands in contrast to exact but slow algorithms. Imagine a game, for example, which computes interactions on a molecular level. The physico-chemical simulation would be exact. Nevertheless, the player would freak out because the game would update the screen only every few minutes.

> *Approximation, fakery and abstraction are vital for games.*

Hollywood, the cousin of the game industry, creates illusions by shallow facades, smoke and mirrors. Building real cities for town shots or scrapping dozens of real vehicles in car chases would be way too expensive. So they fake it. And it works. The same goes for games. Leave out every detail on assets which won't be seen at any camera angle. Bake procedural particle effects into simple sprite animations. Use approximating algorithms instead of realistic ones.

In many cases it's better to ignore school wisdom (i.e. correctness) and do what simply works. A working shortcut is often enough.

## Time Estimation Hell

One of the biggest problems in game development, and in software project management in general, is time estimation. The question of how long it will take to implement a specific task is a horror for many coders and artists. Often, it's estimating how long something will take which you have never done before. Where should you get this knowledge from? You would need to have a similar task already completed to make an educated guess. It's a chicken-and-egg problem.

ASD tries to circumvent this problem by breaking down software design into its core and extending parts. The core should be as small as possible so that it can be tested as early as possible. The extensions get added as long as there is time and money left.

Now we have the homogeneous core which still needs to be estimated. The problem isn't gone, but it became smaller and less threatening.

To get estimable tasks, make them as small and simple as possible. I would even suggest reducing them to primitiveness. If you have an online game, for example, which needs a nickname for each player: generate it. Don't let the player enter it. Don't plan a credential system if you don't have to. Just throw a random yet unique name at the player and let him play. When it needs to be more complicated than this: so be it. But you may get away with the primitive version. This happens more often than you think.

Small and simple tasks have the advantage that they can be accomplished within a few hours. If you are not used to task estimation yet, try to break some tasks down into sub-tasks of less than an hour. When you implement them you may be surprised how long even the tiniest task can take. Another insight for newbies is the "sponginess" of some tasks. "Is it done now or not?" It's important to define your tasks properly. Define what the task's result is and what isn't. Otherwise it's free for interpretation and you hardly know when it's done. Imagine yourself instructing somebody else. Maybe you really have to instruct a team member. The more precise you are, the better and faster the result will be.

After a while in the cycle of task division and implementation, you will get a feeling for what is an hour task and what's a day task. And that's everything you need. The core of most games should be playable within a few weeks (yes, that's doable – just focus on the core mechanic and cut out graphics, sounds and other "fancy stuff"). Therefore there can't be that many tasks you will have to estimate for the core. Avoid estimating future tasks. This is especially true for the extension parts. ASD makes ever-changing adventures out of software projects. Thus don't waste too much time estimating far-off tasks which easily become obsolete.

# Prematurity

This section discusses several problems of tackling issues before they really become issues. This sounds a little bit strange. Nevertheless, it happens quite often. Coders, designers and artists spot flaws in their workings and tend to fix them immediately. That sounds like a good idea. So why should that be a problem? Well, there is always the economical question: does it pay off? Premature work often results from gut feeling instead of proper consideration. Without consulting the bigger picture, premature work quickly becomes counterproductive.

## Premature Optimization

Donald Knuth, a pioneer of computer science, once said:

*"Premature optimization is the root of all evil."*

This quote addresses the problem that optimization often affects the design and the readability of source code. On the one hand it improves the execution speed of a program. On the other hand, it increases the cost for maintenance and debugging. It's an economical question: does the speedup outweigh the higher complexity?

When it comes to software optimization, rookies can easily be distinguished from the pros. The former guess which code is slow and jump right into fixing it. The latter measure what's slow, ponder several solutions and apply the best one.

> Do you feel exposed as an optimization rookie? Don't worry. I have been one for over a decade, unknowingly.

Now, how can software be optimized?

There are multiple levels of optimization. The most important level is the software design. It's all about architecture and choosing the right algorithms. This has the biggest effect on the overall performance. The next optimization level is the source code. This is where programmers spend most of the day. Therefore it seems to be the most promising area for optimization. The truth is: most compilers are better at optimizing code for their target platforms than most programmers. The same is true for the assembly level. Nowadays the messing around with assembly language is a forsaken art. Modern compilers apply the optimization knowledge of several decades to your program. Therefore it makes more sense to use the best tools for optimization instead of doing it yourself.

> I consider choosing the right languages and tools to be a separate optimization step. It can speed up coding, debugging and code execution tremendously.

Program flaws often unfold only at runtime. This is especially true for speed issues. Only profiling, the measurement of execution times, can tell you where bottlenecks are located. Don't guess where code could be slow. Measure where it is actually slow. Also think twice if you really need a specific optimization. Fix it only if it becomes a problem for the player. Not for you, for the player.

## Premature Game Design

Hardly any initial game design makes it to the end. Ideas which initially seem innovative and fun often just turn out to be boring or don't work at all.

You won't be able to come up with a working game design on the first attempt unless you have quite some game design experience under your belt. Even seasoned designers need to field-test their ideas to wipe out the bad seed. So spending a long time in the *game design ivory tower*, pondering features, mechanics and graphics styles for the ultimate game doesn't work. It's vital to test ideas for their potential under real world conditions as soon as possible. Otherwise you run the risk of spending months on an idea which has no chance of survival.

When you have finally found a potential game idea, field tests are still necessary. Premature game design happens when you start detailing aspects of your game too soon. Designing an inventory management, for example, may become pointless when it's not certain that the items will actually be in the game. Considering multiplayer aspects in a single-player game to avoid "spoiling that possibility" is expensive wishful thinking. The control scheme for a lock pick feature becomes worthless when there are no locked doors in the final version. The latter sounds silly. Nevertheless, such mistakes are made.

The root of the premature design problem is the "wouldn't it be cool if..." thought. Some ideas are so tempting that designers integrate them without thinking twice. Games are all about feelings. About the *player's* feelings, to be exact. Newbie game designers often misinterpret the "wouldn't it be cool if..." feeling with the "this is fun to play" feeling. When you know the difference between the two feelings, half the battle against premature game design is won.

## Premature Promises

Don't promise 100s of different weapons and dozens of levels for your game before you have made any of them. Only when you know how long it takes to design, draw, implement, test and polish your game's elements can you estimate how much you can achieve with your budget.

The better solution is to promise nothing at all. It just restricts your freedom before you know if you can keep your word.

> The first game I really wanted to publish had the

working title *Bionic*. It was an adventure game in isometric view like *Baldur's Gate*. The core feature was the main character's artificial limbs, which were exchangeable. The initial game design proposed dozens of different arms, hands, weapons, legs and feet. My enthusiasm let me promise thousands of limb combinations to my followers. A bad idea.

What I hadn't taken into consideration during design was that each limb needed animations for eight different views (due to the isometric view) multiplied by the number of different actions like walking, climbing, item usage, etc. The effort escalated exponentially. Even cutting back the number of limbs did not help. It was just too much work. Stripping the limb feature was a KO criterion for the game. Despite this fact the romantic vision of the finished game kept me working on it for about 3 years before I gave in.

As you may guess, *Bionic* never saw the light of day.

## Premature Feature Integration

Sometimes, when coding a new interface (in terms of source code), it's tempting to do more than necessary. The underlying engine provides sprite rotation, for example. When it's there, why shouldn't rotation be brought to the *Knight* class interface? It's so easy. Let's do it. Everything you do have is good.

Forget it. First of all: a wider interface needs more testing. Then there will be effects on the implementation of the *Knight* class. For instance, there are armor and weapons a knight can hold. You have to rotate them as well. What about collision detection? The rotation has to be taken into account for collisions too. And so on and so forth.

Each new feature introduces new dependencies and therefore more work. All this extra effort for a feature you *may* use one day.

Don't add a skin color slider to your character creation just because the underlying engine enables it out of the box. Don't add terrain-specific attacks just because it's possible. Forget implementing multiple weapon slots when you've planned only one weapon per character.

> The initial design of my shoot 'em up game *Nordenfelt* included multiple battle ships with different weapon slot layouts. Today *Nordenfelt* has just one battle ship with one equipment slot. Implementation and tests for ship selection, handling multiple slots and other functionality were for the birds.

Wait a minute! Premature feature integration sounds just like premature game design, doesn't it? That's true. Both result in features which may never be used. The difference is that premature design brings out unnecessary work from the game designer while premature features come from the coder. The former goes top-down while the latter goes bottom-up.

## Premature Polish

An example of premature polish is completing an asset's initial design without testing the design in the game. A combat mech may look great as a sketch but may not fit into the game due to several reasons. The mech's shape may not align to the overall design concept. Its size could be too large or the shape may result in problematic animations.

Testing assets as rough drafts in your game saves time. Sometimes the rough version is already enough, for example for fast-paced backgrounds. On the other hand you can wipe out inappropriate assets early in the development process.

> When I started working on my steampunk shoot 'em up game *Nordenfelt*, I published all my progress on its blog. One step in *Nordenfelt's* asset creation process was modeling vehicles in 3D for rendering them as 2D sprites. I felt convinced in making the models good-looking on the blog. Following the steampunk theme, I added details like pipes, folds, rivets and grunge to make the models look cool in close-up view. As you may guess, these details took a very long time. Then, when I rendered the models as sprites and scaled them down to in-game size, I realized that hardly any details were visible. All the polish work was all for nothing. It made for nice close-ups for the blog but did nothing for the game.

Polish should only be allowed for assets which are guaranteed a place in the game. The same is true for any type of feature. Don't polish a turd.

## Stamp Design

Before I got into writing games, I attended a school for interior design and architecture. There I learned how to design homes, restaurants and stores, which all follow the same procedure. First, you have to come up with the room layout. In interior construction language, this means figuring out where the walls are, where doors and windows are located, measuring room heights, etc. After gathering these limits, you start designing the floor plan. In this regard, the most important advice from our teachers was to limit our sketches to the size of stamps. The advantage of this restriction is that there is no chance of getting lost in details. Positioning furniture or installations at such a small size is hardly possible and pointless anyway.

This trick is applicable for game design as well. Sometimes it's hard to keep one's hands off pleasing detail work like drawing sprites, improving enemy behaviour or fiddling around with special effects. Staying focused on formal, theoretical work can be tough. It's grinding, actually, working through tasks you don't like.

The stamp size limit can be used in any tier of a design process. In architecture, after figuring out the floor plan in stamp size, each room again can be roughly designed with stamp sized sketches. Game design has these tiers too. The following list is an example of the design tiers of a generic FPS game:

- Rough background story
- Story details per chapter
- Missions derived from chapters

- Level maps derived from missions
- Buildings, interior, vegetation and other assets in levels
- Design of the level assets

While working on any of these tiers, the tier below should be ignored. Limit your design space, either by a maximum number of words used to describe a story or a restricted size for sketches and layouts. This way, the next tier is hard to touch. There is just enough space for the details in the current tier.

# Mastering Emotions

Emotions can be dangerous in game development. Decision-making based on gut feeling leads your game project towards your very own preferences. This sounds good at first. It is good if your project is only a hobby. But if you want to make money, there are more important emotions than your own which you have to consider: the emotions of your audience. That does not mean yours are unimportant. It's just a question of setting priorities.

Here is an example. Choosing fun tasks over necessary tasks is an emotional problem. Everybody understands that work should be fun and motivational. But the focus should lie more on the results and less on the path leading to them. Otherwise you will have fun until you realize that there is no progress. This is the point when fun is superseded by demotivation. A simple solution to this problem would be taking on tasks as they come. This way, fun and struggle will merge.

This section touches on common emotions which can easily overwhelm game makers.

## Motivation

Motivation is the mental fuel for success. Neither an extensive set of skills, nor the best equipment, nor an abundant budget will take your project to the finish line when all your motivation has gone down the drain.

### *Facilitate Your Initial Motivation*

Usually people are bursting with energy when they start with a new project. They can't wait to get cracking. This motivation comes from the desire for creation, to bring a vision into reality. At the beginning you can't get your idea out of your head. It wants you to get started. This drive is the same which keeps you going when things get complicated. I guess everyone who has ever started making a game knows this feeling of being highly motivated.

Fatigue is the natural enemy of motivation. It arises when tasks never get completed. Keeping projects short is a good way to prevent yourself from suffering from fatigue. The longer they take, the higher is the risk of losing momentum, that is to say, leaking motivation.

Take the following as a rule of thumb for scheduling your game projects:

> *Don't let your project see the same season twice.*

In other words: get it done within a year. If you take the usual misestimation factor into account (some say it's PI), your initial schedule for the game should fit into a quarter of a year. The inevitable delay resulting from unexpected problems and unconsidered efforts will make it expand to a year anyway. The less game development experience you have, the shorter your project should be. You can go bigger anytime.

Another piece of advice for keeping your motivation high is choosing your project wisely. You may have several game ideas to choose from. Which one do you really want to make? There can be several reasons. One is the outcome. Maybe it's an interesting idea like a mix of *Battlefield* and *Braid*. Wouldn't it be cool if you were the designer of such a game? Another reason can be the path to the goal. Which works do you enjoy and which do you hate? Find out which tasks you really like and choose a project which promises them. Bear in mind: you will work quite some time on the game. Deciding on an action game would be counter-productive if you are into strategy games. Finally, it's helpful to know if there are similar games out there. If you want to make decent money from your game, it would be foolish to enter a crowded genre.

## *How to Stay Motivated*

The initial motivation, as explained above, won't continue forever. It depletes as your project progresses. That's natural because transforming theoretical ideas into reality undergoes some friction. This means that many of the shiny features of your idea won't be doable in reality. A procedurally-generated storyline, for example, won't be as interesting as a handcrafted one. It's more likely to be boring, repetitive and generic. Additionally, as you implement your game, problems will pop up by the dozen. Each new bump in the road of development "helps" to diminish your motivation.

To avoid running out of motivation, it's good to have some tricks at hand to revive it. The following list shows tricks how to rekindle the flame of enthusiasm:

- **Cut off distractions:** Turn off your email client, your phone and, if you need it hardcore, unplug the Internet. Motivation is fragile and can fall to pieces if you are disrupted continuously.

- **Jump right into it:** Hesitating to get going with uninspiring tasks is often the only obstacle which separates you from motivation. It builds up as you go. Just start without thinking. Start slowly, start poorly if necessary and feel your motivation rise.

- **Quotes:** Pin your favorite motivational quotes to your wall right in front of you at your workplace or use them as screensaver. I prefer the screensaver method because it moves. Things that don't move get ignored easily.

- **People:** Talk with other people about your lack of motivation. They may have some words of encouragement for you. Others may be an inspirational source for you to go on. If you are working in a team, motivation can come from group members as well. But don't overdo the lamenting within your team. It may ruin the shared work morale.

- **Rest:** Sometimes it just needs a night of good sleep

to get back on track. Rest regularly to recharge your batteries. Take a day off. If a day doesn't help, consider going on a short vacation.

- **Exercise:** When you stress your muscles, your brain can roam. I use the word "roam" instead of "rest" because the human brain never rests. There is always something going on in there. Thus, ideas come easily when you are not pondering. Your motivation gets recharged when you can forget your troubles for a short time. Think in terms of a mind vacation.

- **Deal with setbacks:** Your enthusiasm can come to a halt quickly when you get negative feedback or fail somehow. Sit back and distance yourself from the setback. Sleep on it and find the lesson in it. Even the hardest setbacks bear opportunities you may not have recognized yet. Find them.

- **Resolve overload:** Sometimes it's just a cluttered schedule which depletes your drive. Do only one thing at a time. Tidy up your to-do list and focus on the most important task you have to do right now. Everything else is secondary.

- **Expose yourself:** Tell others what you want to achieve and when. This will make you stick to it. To make it even juicier: make a bet. Set up a date when you plan to have a specific milestone accomplished. Then give a certain amount of money to a friend and instruct him to donate it to an organization you dislike when you miss the deadline. This way it becomes real punishment if you let it slide.

- **Meditation aka visualization:** Sit quietly for a few

minutes, relax and ask yourself "What do I really want?" Let the answer come by itself, regardless what it may be. When you have the answer, imagine which actions you have to take to get what you desire. Then imagine the first step and start doing it. This process can take some time until you get a clear vision of what you have to do. Don't rush it. It's better spending a few hours on clarifying your goals and actions than wasting months heading into the wrong direction.

Consult this list whenever you feel demotivated. Read through it, pick a piece of advice and fuel your motivation with it. Everybody has a different approach to motivate himself. Not all advice works for everyone. Try them and find out what works best for you.

## Procrastination

Humans love to delay decisions. This is because making a decision is often taking up a position, a statement, which other people can then criticize. So a decision yields the threat of being attacked by others.

A common example is postponing release dates. The decision that your game's current version is ready for the public is a statement which can be attacked. What will they think about it? Is it good enough? These questions can make you feel uncomfortable about going public. So you add a "game changing" feature or improve some graphics to make it releasable. After that, the same questions arise and you spend yet another week improving the game. This cycle can go on for a very long time.

The chapter *Accept Imperfection* has the cure to fight this feeling. Your game will never be perfect. Therefore, you can release it anytime. Nowadays, people are aware that software is updated regularly. They will not complain when the first version of your game is in beta state or even in alpha. Just let them know what they can expect and deliver it.

Decisions underlie the rule of habit. The more decisions you make, the easier it gets. In particular, experiencing the fact that hardly any decision is written in stone makes it easier to shoot from the hip.

So: decide often and decide now!

## Embarrassment Happens

Do any of the following thoughts sound familiar to you?

- "My game does not look as good as I had in mind."
- "The gameplay does not work as expected."
- "It sucks compared to game X."

Usually these thoughts come up just before you want to release your game. It's the anxiety of getting shot down in flames which lets them bubble up in your mind. The fear of possible harm from the Internet community alone makes you feel embarrassed.

There is one fact that makes dealing with embarrassment easier:

*People forget very fast.*

Publish your game as it is, receive some good reviews and feedback (people are not that picky), receive some bashing (some people are always picky) and fade into obscurity (people forget). Repeat this a few times and the embarrassment will go away. Fight this emotion by knowing that you just fear the worst case scenario. Do it a few times and you will see that the worst case never happens. Well, almost never.

Matt Mullenweg, the founder of *Wordpress*, once said:

> *"If you are not embarrassed when you ship your first version, you waited too long."*

It's reassuring to know that even successful people are embarrassed sometimes.

## Feedback: Cure and Curse

Software development relies heavily on user feedback. At least it should. Therefore you will have to deal with many different opinions about your game, both positive and negative. Getting good reviews, on the one hand, is always nice. Bad reviews, on the other hand, can really drag you down.

First of all you have to know:

> *Everything has fans and enemies.*

Check out any fast-selling goods on *Amazon*. The more reviews there are, the higher the chance is that somebody shares his particular dislike. I would even go so far as to say that good stuff *must* have enemies. The question is not if your game is disliked by somebody but what its like/dislike ratio is.

Feedback is necessary to steer your game project in the right direction. But don't overdo the feedback integration. Not everything that's essential in the eye of a player is really good for your game. Following each piece of advice leads nowhere.

*Try to satisfy everybody and you will satisfy nobody.*

Always ask yourself if a suggested feature really fits into your game (vision) and if it's important. Don't trip over fixing tester-detected bugs immediately. Emotions of emergency and accommodation should not dictate your work. For this, it's helpful to dump all feedback on a list first and let emotions settle. Then sort the feedback by importance. Issues which get mentioned again and again should bubble up on the list. Always tackle the most important point first and update the list regularly.

You will receive constructive critiques as well as destructive ones. Take the former, leave the latter. If somebody just wants to run you down without providing valuable information for improvement, you are safe to put this person on your black list. It is just a waste of time listening to such folk.

## The First Step Is the Hardest

Doing a new type of task for the first time is tough. You barely have a clue what to do and how to do it right. There are so many unknown factors which can feel quite daunting. Here are a few examples of first-time situations:

- Releasing your first game.
- Drawing 2D sprites for the first time.
- Sending out the first email to newsletter subscribers.
- Charging for a game for the first time.
- Writing your initial press release.

Going back to work you already know seems very tempting in these situations. It's your comfort zone which calls you back. Sometimes this call is enough to procrastinate an uncomfortable task and do something else instead.

Taking the first step is hard. Postponing it is easy.

There is a trick to overcome the fear of getting started with something new: start without thinking about it. The longer you ponder the possible outcome, the harder it gets. The primal part of your brain wants to dissuade you from entering uncharted waters because it may be dangerous. When you are in the wilderness this can save your life. In game development this can only save you from success. After plunging into a new challenge at the deep end without preliminary consideration, you will realize that it's not as bad as it seemed "from the outside". It's just unfamiliar.

Another trick is to get rid of the illusion of perfectionism. Nothing is perfect and nothing has to be. Author G.K. Chesterton even went so far as to say:

*"If a thing is worth doing, it is worth doing badly."*

This quote means that you don't have to be a professional to do what's good or important. Raising firstborn kids, for example, is an endeavor generally carried out by amateurs: freshman parents. Apparently, evolution has no demand for perfectionism. Evolution is the keyword here. Don't consider a first attempt as the final one. It's just the first step in a series of steps which will lead to a new skill.

Successful people don't think "I can't do that". They just start doing it and continue to do it until they have mastered it. Most people are worried they will blame themselves along the way. Don't get held back by this anxiety. Rather, concentrate on the envisioned outcome and you will achieve it. The thought of blame is lost quite fast.

## Start Somehow

Creative people, like painters, authors or designers sometimes suffer from *blank canvas fear*. This is when the mind goes blank while facing a blank sheet of paper or a pristine canvas. Ideas stop bubbling up and there is no chance to get a workflow started. Often, this is just a temporary halt which can be solved with a handful of tricks.

Ideas can't be forced. They only emerge naturally from inspiration which can come from many sources like reading books, watching movies or having interesting discussions. It also comes from having an idle mind, e.g. while taking a shower or going for a walk or run.

If ideas still don't come, despite of interesting input or straying thoughts, steal. I'm not referring to taking away something from another person. Just copy what's already there. If you can't get a new endboss design going, for example, search the Internet for images of other endbosses for inspiration. Watch videos of bosses, copy what already works in other games and adapt it for your own game. This is way faster than pulling new, yet-to-be-tested behaviour, sounds and graphics out of thin air. It may not be a novel endboss. But it's a tried and tested one. And you can always alter it to your likings.

Stealing, in this regard, is just a trick to get started quickly.

> When it comes to the *starting somehow*, I like the map metaphor. Pondering on the best start is like searching for the highest peak (i.e. best solution or design) on an endless map. When you start somehow, on the other hand, you start at a random point on the map and try to find the highest peak in proximity. You may not find the highest peak, aka the best solution, there. But at least it's a starting point, just to get your flow gain momentum.

*Starting somehow* can be used for any design purpose, like character design, AI scripting, level prototypes or game mechanics. *Blank canvas fear* can also happen when you start making a game. You may get stuck in the preparation phase. This is common for game dev newbies, who keep updating their design documents, refining not yet implemented mechanics and laying out level maps without a clue how the whole game will evolve. All this is just procrastination of real game development. The cure is to start somehow, with a prototype. It can be ugly, bug-infested and boring. Yet it's worth much more than the shiniest design document because it leads to active development.

Don't mistake *starting somehow* for skipping plans. Planning is good. Nevertheless, there are times when you just can't find the right access point to a task. This is the time to *start somehow*. Get into the flow of working on the task as fast as possible, regardless of the initial value you may create. The rest will unfold naturally.

## Price Shame

A common emotional problem in selling games is setting a price. On the one hand, it should make as much money as possible. On the other hand, a high price feels greedy. So what is the right price for your game?

First of all you have to know your market. If you sell a game on the *App Store* or on *Google Play* you have to go free-to-play or sell it for under $3. Only about 5% of all game apps sell for more than $3. Unique strategy games for PC, however, can sell for $15 or more. AAA blockbuster games sell for more than 50 bucks. But you aren't working on an AAA game, are you?

> The numbers above were valid at the end of 2013. I assume they won't get better than this.

Now that you have an idea what your market and its price range are you can search for games similar to your own. If you have problems finding similar games I congratulate you. You seem to have something unique at hand. In this case, you can try the upper limit of your market's price range. If you find plenty of similar games, you will have to go to the lower limit of the price range.

A rule of thumb: the more similar games, the lower the price.

Now comes the economical part. You have to know what your total production costs are. This includes programming, design, graphics, audio, marketing and all other expenses which can be assigned to your game. Then you divide the costs by the chosen price and see how many sales you need to cover your costs. Don't forget that middlemen also take their share.

The problem with the production costs is that you can't estimate them without according experience. Therefore you can't calculate the number of necessary sales. Only your game on sale can bring you this knowledge. You can find some game sales statistics on the Internet but they are hardly applicable for your own game. Each project is different.

This chicken-and-egg problem has a disappointing solution: you have to test the water with a small game which doesn't need to cover its production costs. Experiment with its price over time and find the maximum income. When you have a free-to-play game the same goes for in-app purchases. Try to market the game until it breaks even. If it fails, you know at least what does not work. There is no better way than learning by doing.

Last but not least: don't get affected by complaints about high prices. It's the customer's job to go for the lowest price. Your job, however, is to get the highest income. Customers are highly reactive. So you will see what they are willing to pay by your sales statistics, not by angry emails or criticizing reviews. Rely on facts, not on feelings.

The price is always a question of supply and demand and not of how you feel about it. So there's no need to feel ashamed about a price. Not finding your optimal price is shameful at best.

## Don't Take It Personally

In private life, as well as in a professional career, you will face critique and insults. They hurt emotionally. And they will make your thoughts spin around the question "I am as bad as they say?"

Have you ever talked to somebody about these feelings, just to get confronted with "don't take it personally"? That sounds much easier than it's done. How to not take something aimed at you or your game personally? That would be like getting shot and trying to not feel the bullet.

In contrast to the getting-shot metaphor, critique and insults are not lethal. They are just words which can't harm you, at least not physically. It's just your brain which transforms the words into something offensive. The good thing is that your brain can be trained to react differently.

### *Brain Reeducation Step #1*

Give the benefit of the doubt. Maybe people are just joking around or have a bad day. Your instinct may tell you to react emotionally, but pause for a second. Maybe it's not about you or the game you're working on. Don't jump to conclusions too early.

People also may have poor communication skills and their inner child acts out. When somebody insults you or butchers your game, imagine this person as child who is still learning how to behave. That way it's easier to be patient and to distance yourself from apparent offense.

## *Brain Reeducation Step #2*

In the same way that you should not take critique or insults personally, you should stop taking compliments personally too. If you base your self-worth on other people's compliments you become dependent on other people's opinions. Compliments, critique and insults are siblings. Compliments don't make you a better person; they make the *complimenter* a better person. The same is true for insults. They don't make you a bad person. They just reflect what others can't deal with. Your value remains unchanged, neither affected by compliments nor insults.

Compliments, critique and insults only show how others see you. If you get many compliments, you seem to have something people resonate with. On the other hand, if you get criticized often, folks don't resonate with your opinion or deeds. Either you are on a wrong track or just into something polarizing. Clarification is king in the latter case. To understand, if you have to take specific critique seriously, it's necessary to get a clear concept of what's "wrong". If, for example, critique about graphics comes from eye-candy spoiled gamers, you can ignore it unless you are in the eye-candy gamer maker business. If it's a proper analysis of your gameplay which points out major flaws, you should take it seriously and thank the author for it. Honest and constructive feedback is vital for improving games.

### *Brain Reeducation Step #3*

The last brain education step is a simple one. Let emotions settle. Wait a little while before you deal with new critique. This way your judgment will be more objective and goal-oriented. Professional sports teams do the same. After a match, they don't discuss what went well or what went wrong. They calm down and review the match a day later.

## Emotions Equal Sales

In contrast to the foregone chapters, this chapter is not about dealing with emotional issues of game development. It's about marketing and how it utilizes the emotions of customers. So, let's see how customer brains work.

We humans think we are intelligent creatures, in full control of our thoughts and led by rational decisions. This couldn't be farther from the truth. Emotions control most of our behaviour. Our intellect is just allowed to veto after a decision was made by instinct. We are still apes, after all.

Emotions are reactions, based on integral knowledge, hard-wired into our brains. They tell us right from wrong, with reflex-like speed. Now think of this: what if you could trigger specific emotions in other people's brains to influence them? Sounds weird? It is. This is the point where marketing comes into play.

Officially, marketing is communicating the value of products and services to customers so that they spend money on them. Put bluntly, the real core of marketing is psyche exploitation. Let's take a car advertisement, for example. The value of a car comes from the quality of its parts, their assemblage, the design and its features. Yet, ads ignore most of these points. Instead, they show some smiling guy driving along a coast road at sunset, suggesting that this car brings its driver the feeling of freedom. This is old marketing wisdom at work: facts tell, but emotions sell. In other words: facts tell, stories sell. Have you ever wondered why religious books and mythology tell their wisdom as stories of saints and deities? They could reduce their message to a set of propositions and rules instead.

Rules are meant to be broken. Idols get imitated.

When David Darling, co-founder of *Codemasters*, was asked how he thinks the game industry has changed since the 80s, he answered:

> *"It's about human feelings, and they don't really change."*

Like the car buyer, who decides for the ragtop instead of the more reliable family van, people choose games which tickle their emotions. They don't buy due to logical reasoning, but due to how the game makes them feel.

Armed with this piece of knowledge, marketers have been investigating the human mind for many centuries now. Marketing became the art of bypassing the rational mind and infiltrating the vulnerable yet mighty amygdala, the brain's center of emotion.

Drug designers do the same. Just saying.

If your game or its advertisement can tell a poignant or funny story, you have won half the battle. Think about viral content on the Internet. Most shares involve fun, social connection, horror or sex. This list isn't complete, but you get the idea.

The lesson is clear: serve the player's emotions and you will earn big bucks. *World of Warcraft* and other MMORPGs have close to perfect addiction traits. Some people got so hooked, they died from playing for too long without food and sleep. That's the dark side of the *Force*.

# Everyday Life Hacks

This last section addresses tricks for everyday life. Many lessons from game development can also be used for personal growth and vice versa. Often good things from one discipline can be adopted for other disciplines. Subtractive design, for example, can be applied to game design, to martial arts or to cooking. A short explanation of subtractive design is "reducing a design or plan to a minimum to strengthen its core". In game design, this would be removing features which are not necessary for the core gameplay. In martial arts, it would be perfecting a minimum set of techniques. For cooking, subtractive design means focusing on simple, nutritious, yet delicious, meals.

Everyday life hacks should be used on a daily basis. This way they become second nature and improve your mindset for game development and any other work. Everything incorporated in your subconscious mind works on autopilot. So you can focus on the work you have to do, not on how you do it.

## Knowledge Is worth Nothing

You may have heard this proverb before:

*Knowledge is power.*

This phrase is attributed to Francis Bacon who lived from 1561 to 1626. At that time, only the wealthy were educated which therefore had the power over the illiterate folks. Today, in the information age, everyone has access to the knowledge of the world. Nevertheless, there is a powerful minority and the powerless majority. So why is that? Is it the difference in education? It isn't. The proverb has just lost its validity in our modern society. It needs a little update:

*Applied knowledge is power.*

It does not matter if you know everything about a topic. If you don't apply your knowledge, you won't be successful in this domain. Practice what you preach. Or rather practice what you *know*. This is especially true for the content of this book. If you just read through it and never apply at least one of the concepts, you just bought a new dust catcher for your book-shelf.

Theoretical wisdom without practice is just useful for braggarts.

## Discipline

Discipline is a very important characteristic of successful people. Aside from the craftsmanship that your work demands, it's vital to get a grip of yourself. The last sentence may sound a little harsh. Usually discipline is seen as stressing specific behaviour. The bad word here is "stressing". It has this negative connotation. People don't want to be forced, stressed or have to leave their comfort zones. Therefore they don't want discipline.

The good news is that discipline is not about keeping specific behaviour up in difficult situations. It's about repeating something regularly until it becomes second nature. Discipline is about adopting traits by simple repetition. When something has become second nature, there is no longer the need to think about it. You just do it.

If you want to acquire a new skill or behaviour start small, simple and repeat it regularly. Do it daily, weekly or at any other interval you are comfortable with. Examples would be getting fit, learning to draw sprite art, learning new tools or learning to play a new instrument. There is only one rule: keep doing it until it's natural to you. When you do it automatically, you've reached your goal. Humans are creatures of habit. So why not exploit this loophole by installing wanted skills through repetition? Let good things creep into your life in small doses.

> I can't tell you when I started doing pushups regularly. Many years have passed by since then. The only thing I know is that I was able do 20 fast ones in the beginning.

> I thought that wasn't too bad. But then I saw this guy in the gym doing 50 pushups *after* lifting heavy weights at the butterfly machine. At that moment I decided to get better at it. So I set the goal doing pushups *every day* for two weeks. To zest the plan I decided to do at least one additional pushup every day. After fourteen days I was able to do more than 40 pushups.
>
> Effect 1: Pushups became a habit, not a hassle.
>
> Effect 2: Bye bye, flat chest.

## Health

Ah, the usual "live healthy" chapter. I guess you've encountered this topic already if you are curious about self-improvement in any regard. The point is: a healthy life is the basis for good working conditions. The following proverb from Roman poet Juvenal puts it straight:

*"A sound mind (lives) in a healthy body."*

The first point, obviously, is a healthy diet. You are what you eat. I think you know what to do. Reduce the baddies like fried stuff and sugar and eat more of the goodies like vegetables and fruit.

The second point is physical training. Go for a run, ride your bicycle or lift weights. Any exercise helps.

Many people fail to follow this advice because they are highly motivated at the beginning and jump right into eating 100% healthily and working out like crazy in the gym. Soon they get back into their old habits, get demotivated and give up flagging it as "too hard for me". Sure, it's too hard to change all your habits overnight. Ignore those TV shows which show you how to crucify yourself in the name of getting in shape. Forget the before and after photos. And please, don't do drugs to get in shape.

Do the following instead: start slowly. If you don't do any fitness yet, start with something simple like pushups, a short run or a walk around the block. Do just a few pushups per day and raise the number the next day. Increase the distance of your walks or runs. Add a second training set to your pushups, e.g. weight lifting. If you are a walker, try running as well. Just for 10 minutes. Then run longer. You don't have to go to a gym if you don't want to. But if it motivates you, go there. Motivation is the key. As long as you keep exercising within your limits, motivation will come naturally.

The same applies to food. Eat one piece of fruit or vegetable per day. Then do without one piece of candy a day. Put sweets and other unhealthy stuff away where you can't see them. Not buying it in the first place is the best solution. Incorporate the healthy food into your daily diet step by step. Eat lean meat, drop refined grain like flour, replace simple sugar with complex sugar like honey. And, for god's sake, replace soft drinks with water. Consuming junk food every once in a while is no problem. Just keep "every once in a while" period longer than a week.

> I love coffee and meat, as many people do. I could not imagine living without them. The vitalizing feeling after the first morning coffee was just too good to quit. A meal without meat wasn't a full meal to me.
>
> Today I'm vegetarian and drink coffee only occasionally. Why? Coffee makes for yellow teeth, bad breath and gives me a headache after the $3^{rd}$ cup. Tea doesn't. The reason why I switched to vegetarianism is a philosophical one: I want to live without factory farming. A pleasant side effect to being reduced to healthy food is that it makes living healthily easy. I'm not against eating meat. I'm just against inappropriate husbandry.
>
> I still love meat and coffee. Nevertheless, I removed them from my diet plan, step by step. Little strokes fell big oaks, even the ones you really like.

Aside from going for a better fitness level, there are tricks to improving your health in the office. Rest your eyes every 1-2 hours for up to 10 minutes. Evolution did not intend for human eyes to be staring into monitor light all day. Get a second monitor to prevent neck strain. Switching between monitors as you work keeps your neck muscles in motion.

Have you ever tried to work standing up? The first attempt will be tiring. But after a few days of practice, you will be able to work without a chair. It's highly recommended for people who suffer from back pain.

The last tip of this chapter is: sleep well. The average person needs 7-8 hours of good sleep. You will feel the lack of concentration when you are sleep-deprived. Take a nap if you didn't get enough sleep. This may sound embarrassing. That's just for toddlers and old people! Think again. Humans are geared towards multiple phases of sleep per day. We just are not used to it anymore because the industrial revolution forced us to stay up in factories and offices all day long. The industrial age is vanishing. Therefore, when you take a nap, be sure to not sleep too long. Sleep only 5-10 minutes, then get up. Set an alarm clock if necessary. If you sleep too long, you will feel like a zombie.

Feel free to have a nap when you get tired. That's one advantage of being self-employed.

## Speed Reading

I assume you are reading books on a regular basis. If you're not, I hope you are reading blogs, magazines or game related news. Otherwise you can skip this chapter, which is the first piece of advice: skip information you don't need.

Still here? Good.

Think about the books you've read so far. How much do you remember from them? Can you recall details of these books? There may be books you know very well because you have read them several times. Other books may need a glance at their indexes to revive their topics in your head. Some books you may have forgotten completely. A look at their cover gives you an idea of what they are about. Yet you can't remember any details.

What I want to point out is that varied information and topics have different significance. To avoid spending time reading information you don't need, it's useful to decide upfront if you want to read it at all. You already do this when you decide if you buy a specific book. So why not apply the same decision process to the book's content? Just because you paid money for it? This may sound ridiculous. Nonetheless, it's a proven fact that people spend more time with things they have paid for than with the same goods for free. This is especially true for free-to-play games and paid games. Guess, which type of game generates more true fans.

Back to speed reading. Decide for each chapter of a book if it's useful for you. The title often tells you what you can expect. Skim over the chapter if the title isn't that descriptive. Go over it from start to end or use the shape technique. The shape technique is simply moving your eyes from the top of the page to its right side, to the page bottom, to the left side and finally back to the top. Don't read the text, just take the words in. Your subconscious mind recognizes more than you consciously are aware of. You can use any figure you want for the shape technique, for instance an S-curve or a diagonal line. After skimming over the first few pages of the chapter, sit back and decide if you are interested in it. If curiosity doesn't arise, you can skip it. You know this chapter is there. Thus, you can come back to it when it becomes useful for you.

The whole process is also known as selective ignorance. It works well for non-fiction books, magazines, blogs, news feeds and other random accessible information. I wouldn't recommend it for novels due to their sequential nature.

OK, wait... Isn't the title of this chapter *Speed Reading*? Where is the advice for *faster reading*?

There are two speed-increasing techniques I can share with you. I just can't say they work. At least they didn't work for me.

The first trick is the *blip page*. Hold an open book in front of you and focus on the center fold. The text should be readable, that is to say, sharp. Then set the focus *behind* the fold, so that you are looking *through* the book. This makes the text blurry. It's like watching those 3D images where suddenly some forms pop out, when you do it right. You should start to see the *blip page*, a seemingly small third page in the middle of the book. This may need some training. When you have got the *blip page*, you still can't read the text. You don't have to either. Just look at the blurry text in the middle for a few seconds, flip the page and do it again. This way the subconscious mind should get an idea of the content. Somehow...

The second trick is *center skimming*. Just read the first few words of each line followed by the last few words of the line. The full meaning should come about automatically. At least they say so...

I could not personally profit from either of these techniques. But maybe you can. If you want to know more about this topic, just search for "speed reading" or

> "photo reading".

## Singleton To-Do List

To-do lists are the backbone of every plan. Grocery lists, *Scrum* backlogs or meeting agendas are examples. They vary in complexity but are basically the same: a list of things to do.

A to-do list in any form is helpful in several regards. It gives you an overview of what you have to do and what's already done. It keeps you on track to pursue your goals. Therefore, it's like a boss who you consult for the next step. To-do lists form the basis for estimations of time and costs. They also give you a sense of progress - how much you have achieved so far. This is a very important aspect, especially for your inner feeling of advancement.

If you're already used to to-do lists, you may face the problem of multiple to-do lists. They come written on sheets of paper, via an issue tracking system, as voice recorded notes, notes on your *iPhone* or sent to yourself by email.

> Heck, I even write to-dos on my lower arms with a ball pen when neither a device nor paper is around.

The distributed nature of multiple to-do lists makes it tough managing them. There always will be a primary list which you spend the most time with. Therefore other to-do lists easily become forsaken. Tasks get lost and reappear on other lists. Simply put, your management backbone becomes scattered and out of sync.

The solution to this problem is simple: use a singleton online to-do list. You can use issue tracking software like *Trac*, to-do list managers like *Wunderlist*, *Evernote*, *Google Drive* or any similar service.

> Whenever there is no Internet access I note ideas and to-dos on paper or write it on my lower arms. To keep everything in sync I've formed the habit of integrating new tasks in my singleton to-do list as soon as I go online.

It's important to maintain just one to-do list. This way you have a one-stop shop from where you can fetch your next task when you're done with the last one. It's so easy to get lost while you're engrossed in work. Thus it's very helpful to have a single golden thread to follow.

## Do First, Learn Later

The modern school system has its roots in the early 20th century when factories had a high demand for compliant workers. Back then, workers were instructed how to perform specific tasks in their work area. It was like programming robots to carry out repetitive tasks.

This is similar to how students are schooled today. There is just one problem: the factories are vanishing. Modern jobs have less and less hackwork but have a high demand for entrepreneurship and autonomy. Entrepreneurs are used to solving problems in an economic manner. This resembles the struggle of real life. Life throws you in the ring and you have to learn the lessons while doing things you have never done before. It's sink or swim. This may sound a little harsh but humans are designed to learn this way.

This bears a huge opportunity. You can accomplish whatever you want, not only what you have learned so far. So you don't have to be instructed by a teacher first to apply new knowledge later. You can happily start what you wanna do right now and learn everything about it along the way. Courses are helpful to shortcut the time you need to get to a certain level. But learning through trial and error, without help from teachers, makes you used to failing and creates confidence when you succeed. Failing is an everyday part of a successful life. So fail often and fail fast. Failure is not weakness. Failures are just steps along the path to success.

Start doing what you want to do even when you have no clue how. Learn what you need when you need it. Do it now and learn on the go.

## Expand Your Comfort Zone

Everything you are used to lies within your comfort zone. This goes for work, school, social connections, partnerships – everything. It's nice and safe in the comfort zone. There is just one problem: if you are not successful, thus success has to be sought after outside of the zone.

*If you keep doing what you're doing you'll keep getting what you're getting.*

This saying is quoted so often that it's hard to trace back who came up with it in the beginning. Anyways, it's not important who said it. It's important what it means. It boils down to the following:

*Try new things to get better.*

Change can come to you or you can come to (the) change. Most people dislike the former, the successful follow the latter.

Experiment with things which you have not done yet or which may even frighten you. Start painting, for example. Learn to program. Participate on a dance course. Talk to strangers. The possibilities are endless and you can only win.

> Maybe talking to strangers is not always a win. There are some crime-infested cities out there...

Experiment on a regular basis. It does not matter what comes out. Pushing the boundary of your comfort zone matters. This way you tap into new territory over and over and therefore lose the fear of entering the unknown. Soon you will enjoy the thrill of the novel. There are just two rules: get it started and get it done. No matter what, finish it. "Nearly done" does not count.

When you tell others about a new project, you may encounter nay-sayers. They will tell you that your undertaking won't work because... Well, because they don't know how it works. Don't listen to people who have no experience in the field you want to try out. They just fear the edge of their own comfort zone. Maybe you have been a nay-sayer yourself. If so, you will understand that they just want to protect you from failure and protect themselves from being left behind by your success.

# About the Author

Thomas Schwarzl is a game developer, author of the book *2D Game Collision Detection*[4] and wannabe digital artist. He resides in the European Alps, right in the heart of Austria.

Writing computer games since 2001 has let Thomas acquire the knowledge how to cope with the inner game of game development. Psychological aspects and especially motivation are rarely discussed game development topics. So it was time to share some wisdom.

After years of employment, writing games for arcade machines, Thomas started the games company *www.blackgolem.com*. Due to being a one-man show, he is involved in every aspect of game development like game design, programming, 2D graphics, 3D modeling and marketing. But his favorite occupation is still cranking out code all night while sipping black tea.

---

4   *www.collisiondetection2d.net*